Kidderminster Town station. New station buildings have been erected by the Severn Valley Railway on the site of the former Great Western Railway goods yard. They were opened to the public on 28th September 1985. The design is based on the former station buildings at Ross-on-Wye and represents the best in GWR practice. The range includes booking hall, bookshop, administrative quarters, and the 'King and Castle' buffet bar. The towers will be capped with iron crestings in French Renaissance style and a new restaurant block will complete the range.

RAILWAY ARCHITECTURE

F. G. Cockman

Shire Publications Ltd

CONTENTS

Printed in Great Britain by C. I. Thomas & Sons (Haverfordwest) Ltd, Press Buildings, Merlins Bridge, Haverfordwest, Dyfed SA61 1XF.

British Library Cataloguing in Publication Data available.

ACKNOWLEDGEMENTS
I am indebted to John Davis for his kind assistance with the photographs. My special thanks go to R. P. Hart RIBA for ensuring the accuracy of the captions, and to Frances, my wife, for her help over the years on our journeys with the camera.
    Photographs are acknowledged as follows: J. J. Davis, page 18 (top); Greater Manchester Museum of Science and Industry, page 2; Cadbury Lamb, pages 7 (top), 10 (top), 11, 22 (bottom), 23, 25, 26 (bottom) and 29; R. H. Marrows, page 1. The remainder are by the author.

COVER: *Ivatt tank number 41316 crossing the Tamar viaduct near Calstock in 1961. The tapered piers give grace and lightness to the structure, which dates from 1908.*

BELOW: *Liverpool Road station, Manchester, was opened on 15th September 1830. After July 1846 the London & North Western Railway diverted traffic to the more convenient station of the Manchester & Birmingham Railway. It is now part of the Greater Manchester Museum of Science and Industry. Note the station agent's house, a typically Georgian building dating from 1806, and, next to it, the imposing first-class booking hall (1830). The entrance flanked by double pilasters and the hooded windows give a most pleasing effect.*

Langley. The original station was built by Brunel in 1840 and when the relief lines were constructed in 1879 the new station was a faithful copy of the original. Note the French pavilion style with trellis ironwork.

INTRODUCTION

The year 1830 saw the beginning of architecture on the railways with the opening of the Liverpool & Manchester Railway. Although the Stockton & Darlington Railway had commenced operations five years previously it was built primarily for the carriage of coal, passengers being conveyed on sufferance for the first few years. The railway promoters realised that a new age of travel had arrived and they wished to impress the public with fine buildings, at least at the termini. To do this they engaged the leading architects of the day, thus passing down to us a large number of excellent buildings. The whole range of well-tried designs was adapted: Greek in its three main orders, Roman, Gothic of various periods, Tudor, Renaissance and Italianate. The last was widely adopted and was of a quality which would have been approved by Canaletto. A large terminal station could be the product of three professionals. The company's engineer would design the large warehouse, today called the trainshed, consisting of an overall roof resting on iron columns, and in this the trains waited to depart for the provinces or arrived therefrom. Passengers were thus sheltered from the weather. Glass panels would be inserted in the roof to light the interior, and as the locomotives burned coke the glass remained reasonably clean for some time. Fortunately, gas lighting had become a commercial proposition by the time the large London stations were ready for use. Next came the station frontage, offices, waiting rooms and booking hall constructed to the designs of an architect and built of stone, or stone and brick, depending on the funds available after the main line had been built. Finally there was the hotel, usually the work of an architect, but often erected a few years after the station had become established. A typical

3

example is Paddington, where in 1854 Brunel placed his admirable transeptal cathedral to serve as a trainshed. The brickwork surrounding, in Elizabethan style, is the work of Digby Wyatt, and finally the Royal Great Western hotel was designed by P. C. Hardwick.

The first terminal stations were very neat, having an arrival platform on the right and a departure platform on the left, the space between being occupied by several tracks and turntables to accommodate empty coaching stock. Examples could be seen at Bristol (Temple Meads) (1841), and King's Cross (1852).

But, as traffic grew, it became necessary to add platforms outside the original building and this rather spoiled the effect, presenting the traveller with a labyrinth of passages. Readers who used the old Waterloo or Euston stations will appreciate the point. Platforms also had to replace the sidings in the trainshed so that the companies had to marshal their trains further away. In London the Great Northern chose Ferme Park, the Midland Welsh Harp, and the London & North Western went to Stonebridge Park. Some stations were unspoiled, such as Fenchurch Street (rebuilt 1853), Charing Cross (1864) and St Pancras (1868).

Competition between the various companies took different forms, among them being the provision of greater comfort at stations. In course of time were added refreshment rooms, waiting-rooms, lavatories and left-luggage offices. With the Victorian addiction to a stratified society the rooms proliferated into first, second and third class waiting, and as these were subdivided between ladies and gentlemen, a terminal station would be saddled with six divisions according to class and sex. The refreshment rooms were sometimes first-class and second-class, or first and third. In the latter case the second-class passenger could make his choice, no doubt preferring to pay the higher prices demanded in the first-class refreshment room for the privilege of being seen entering or leaving it. Finally there was the approach road to the station by means of bridge or tunnel for the arriving and departing cabs, with gentle slopes to ease the work of the horses.

Because Great Britain led the world in railway construction many of the station buildings are now over a hundred years old and therefore are in need of constant repair. Many buildings are of such architectural excellence that they are 'listed', that is to say, they cannot be demolished without the consent of the Department of the Environment. If this consent is not forthcoming, then the building must be preserved. British Rail has limited financial resources for this but fortunately assistance is sometimes given by a local authority.

At St Pancras the brick and stone work was cleaned in 1986 so that it now presents the appearance which it did to the first travellers in 1868. Liverpool Street is to be completely reconstructed but E. Wilson's graceful train shed on the west side, built in 1874, is to be preserved intact. Other London termini, for example London Bridge, Victoria and Paddington, have been greatly improved by increasing the circulating area. This was made possible by shortening the length of the platforms. The modern electric or diesel multiple unit train does not need a locomotive at each end as in steam days, resulting in a saving of space which has been put to good use. Paddington displays an excellent statue of I. K. Brunel.

The adoption of electrification with overhead catenary wires has meant a great deal of rebuilding as all overbridges have had to be raised 6 feet. When this occurred at a station opportunity was taken to restore or renew the buildings. Examples are Northampton, Peterborough, Crewe and Norwich (Thorpe). Oxford, Manchester, Brighton, Leicester and Cardiff have also benefited from reconstruction schemes. Plymouth was completely rebuilt and now has an office block over. Although many thousands of stations disappeared after the Beeching Report of 1963 the trend has been reversed in recent years and several have been reopened. In such cases the practice is to construct a basic station with booking office and staff rooms in concrete with bus-type shelters for passengers.

The many preservation societies have not only restored locomotives and rolling stock to attract the public but have paid great attention to the many buildings in their care. From the North Yorkshire Moors to Sheffield Park in East Sussex, and from Sheringham to Kingswear the station buildings have received expert and loving maintenance.

King's Cross, Lewis Cubitt's twin-arched Romanesque terminus for the Great Northern. The Italianate clock-tower relieves the austerity and now the row of shops has gone we can appreciate the functional beauty of the 1852 design. The GNR boasted that their station cost less than the Doric portico at Euston. Like St Pancras it withstood the onslaught of enemy bombs in 1941.

LONDON TERMINI

The Londoner is fortunate in being able to spend a day inspecting the fifteen terminal stations which so well demonstrate the ability of the Victorian architect. This can be done almost entirely by following the route of the Inner Circle line. It would have been simpler for the traveller, but less interesting to the student, if the companies could have agreed to build one or two stations for joint use, rather like what has been achieved more recently in Rome. Three stations, Fenchurch Street, London Bridge and Victoria, were used jointly, but the nineteenth-century companies were jealous of each other and sharing was not welcomed.

The honour of being first in the capital goes to London Bridge which saw the trains of the London & Greenwich Railway in 1836. The South Eastern and the London & Croydon railways had a joint 'west end' station at Bricklayers Arms in 1844 but this was abandoned and the SER pushed on to Charing Cross in 1864 and to Cannon Street in 1866, both of these fine stations being the work of Sir John Hawkshaw. The London & Birmingham Railway spent a vast sum of money in obtaining an Act for the building of their line, Parliament having rejected the 1832 bill but passing the 1833 bill. However, this did not deter them from spending freely on the erection of the famous Doric propylaeum or portico at the entrance to Euston station in 1837. The architect was Philip Hardwick. Strangely enough, the station was unpretentious.

The new station at Euston was opened by HM the Queen in 1968 but the portico had disappeared in 1962. In his plans dated 1834 Brunel had envisaged a terminus at Vauxhall Bridge, but in 1835 he had changed the site to Paddington, after a proposal to share Euston with the London & Birmingham Railway had been rejected. The temporary GWR station lasted from 1838 to 1854. Also in 1838 the London & Southampton Railway opened their Nine Elms station, the work of Sir William Tite, but the inconvenience of the site made them move on to Waterloo in 1848. Another trunk railway to move was the Great Northern, which deserted its 1850 terminus at Maiden Lane for the beautifully functional King's Cross in 1852. Lewis Cubitt built the station with the same perfection which William Cubitt had shown in laying down the main line to the north. The London Brighton & South Coast Railway opened its part of Victoria station in 1860 and two years later came the London Chatham & Dover Railway. The buildings were extensively altered in 1898.

In 1850 a small railway in north London was opened under the title of the East & West India Docks & Birmingham Junction Railway. It extended to Hampstead Road in 1851 and in 1853 changed its name to the simpler North London Railway. A new terminus was opened at Broad Street in 1865. (The station served north London for 121 years and was closed on 28th June 1986.) Three years later the magnificent St Pancras was opened, but travellers had to wait until 1873 before enjoying the amenities of the hotel. When the Great Eastern Railway was formed in 1862 it found itself with a station at Bishopsgate which had been erected by the Eastern Counties Railway in 1840 to the designs of Sancton Wood and called Shoreditch. The style was attractive Italianate, but it had to be abandoned for Liverpool Street in 1874 to cope with increased traffic. The station was enlarged in 1894 by platforms 11 to 18, constituting the 'east side', to accommodate the increased sub-urban traffic. The architect was W. N. Ashbee. British Rail is involved in an extensive rebuilding scheme which will mean the demolition of the east side and the erection of offices; the west side (1874) will be modernised and will accommodate trains from the former North London Railway. Broad Street station will be demolished and the site redeveloped.

The impecunious LC & DR managed to find the money to build Holborn Viaduct station in 1877, and the last London terminus, Marylebone, was opened in 1899 by the indigent Great Central Railway. This brief summary can be concluded with reference to the Metropolitan Railway, world's first underground. The headquarters at Baker Street dated from 1863 but by 1892 their trains had reached Aylesbury. The consequent increase in traffic necessitated the rebuilding of the London terminus in 1911.

Railway hotels allowed the architect full scope for his genius. Not every London terminus had a hotel attached; there might be lack of space or prohibitive cost. Hardwick introduced baroque at Paddington in 1854 and eleven years later E. M. Barry built two splendid hotels, one at Charing Cross and the other at Cannon Street. Not only did they cater for the comfort of the continental passenger, but both were favourite places for shareholders' annual general meetings. King's Cross was simple but adequate, whereas across the road stood Gilbert Scott's memorable Gothic St Pancras hotel. It opened in 1873 at a cost which alarmed some Midland shareholders, but did its duty well until turned into offices in 1935. Holborn Viaduct once had a hotel and, also in the City of London, the Great Eastern hotel has thriven since 1884. This was the creation of C. E. Barry in Renaissance style. The Great Central spent so much money in building their line to Marylebone that funds were exhausted and the hotel site was leased for others to build upon.

OPPOSITE BOTTOM: *King's Cross Hotel (rear view). The Great Northern Railway moved from their temporary terminus at Maiden Lane (1850) to King's Cross in 1852. There Lewis Cubitt gave them an excellent station for £135,000. Next he was employed to create a hotel and this great building, still thriving, was completed in 1854. It is a mixture of Victorian, Georgian and Neo-Classical, as exemplified by round-topped doors and windows with keystones and six pilasters formed by columns of quoins.*

ABOVE: *Cannon Street. The South Eastern Railway made their expensive move towards the west end of London by opening Charing Cross station in 1864 and Cannon Street in 1866. These replaced the unsuitable Bricklayers' Arms which had been closed to passenger traffic in 1852. An imposing station in Cannon Street was designed by E. M. Barry having campaniles topped by cupolas to blend with the Tower of London. The semicircular roof was damaged during the 1939-45 war and was not reinstated.*

ABOVE: *Fenchurch Street, a splendid building designed by George Berkeley in 1854. Note the Neo-Classical style, with curved pediment and round-topped windows.*

BELOW: *Charing Cross. The austere shed of latticed girders was erected in 1905 when a gale damaged Hawkshaw's roof of 1864.*

Market Harborough. The London & North Western Railway built the first station in 1850 and the Midland arrived in 1857. A new joint station to cope with the increased traffic was opened in 1884. The frontage is very pretty, of excellent Queen Anne design in red brick with stone pilaster strips and dormer window.

PROVINCIAL TERMINI AND JUNCTIONS

The first trunk lines connected important cities and most of the capital was subscribed by city financiers, the intermediate landowners making a much smaller contribution. Accordingly, the citizens of Birmingham expected, and obtained, a grand station in Curzon Street to match Euston. At the northern end of the line Philip Hardwick designed a portico with Ionic columns and it came into use in April 1838, continuing until 1854. In that year, E. A. Cooper built the station at New Street, a short distance away, famous for its great crescent trussed roof 211 feet wide. Curzon Street was then turned over to goods traffic, and fortunately it survives and can be seen from the train as one approaches New Street station from the south. Similar conditions applied at Bristol where Brunel flattered the Great Western directors with

a splendid station at Temple Meads built in Tudor style with convincing mock hammerbeam roof. The GWR opened this station in 1841. Provincial stations which commenced life as terminals often developed into junctions as new lines were built. Examples are at Newcastle (1838), York (1840) and Exeter (1844).

There are so many fine stations worth visiting today that only a small selection can be quoted, and the railway traveller with a keen eye for architecture will make discoveries for himself as he goes about the country. On the LB & SCR, Brighton is a typical example of co-operation between engineer and architect; J. U. Rastrick, who built the railway from Croydon in 1841, designed the trainshed and David Mocatta was responsible for the brick and stone work in the attractive Roman style. H. E. Wallis enlarged the

ABOVE: *Manchester Central was built in 1889 by the Midland Railway jointly with the Cheshire Lines Committee. The roof span of 210 feet is only 30 feet less than St Pancras. Closed in 1969 and used for some years as a car park, the whole site has been taken over for the purposes of the Greater Manchester Exhibition and Event Centre.*

BELOW: *Leicester (Midland). This is the port cochere of the 1892 building which replaced that of 1840. The architect was Charles Trubshaw. The materials are terracotta and swag relieved by red brick. Note the blind doorways with round arches and keystones to relieve the monotony of the brickwork.*

station in 1887. On the North Eastern, in addition to York and Darlington, mention should be made of Hull (Paragon) rebuilt by W. Bell in 1904. As might be expected, the Midland lavished money on Manchester (Central) which was a smaller St Pancras, and on Sheffield which was reconstructed in 1904. As well as New Street, Birmingham had a great station at Snow Hill, built by the GWR in 1909 as a fitting accompaniment to their fine new line from Paddington, only 110½ miles long as compared with the 112½ of the L & NWR.

The twentieth century, before the catastrophe of 1914, saw many excellent stations built or rebuilt in the provinces. Salisbury received attention from the L & SWR in 1900, while Shrewsbury, jointly owned by the GWR and the L & NWR, was enlarged in 1903. Credit must be given to some of the smaller companies for enterprise displayed in building or improving their stations. A case in point is Liverpool (Exchange), first brought into use by the Lancashire & Yorkshire in 1888, while on the other side of the country the Great Eastern, never overburdened with wealth, commissioned the architects J. Wilson and W. Ashbee to reconstruct Norwich (Thorpe). This they did in an excellent Renaissance style in 1886. Just at the turn of the century the Great Central Railway, by opening their

extension to London, built a whole series of stations with island platforms only, the most notable being Leicester and Rugby. This magnificent but unprofitable main line was opened on 15th March 1899.

In Wales, the Chester & Holyhead Railway was opened in 1850, being worked by the L & NWR which absorbed the smaller line in 1858. Holyhead station was enlarged and a hotel built in 1880. The South Wales Railway was an important line having the imprint of Brunel. Swansea (High Street) station was opened in 1850 with trains worked by the GWR, which took over the SWR in 1863. The L & NWR, ever competing with the GWR, ran their first trains into Swansea (Victoria) in 1886. This station has unfortunately been demolished.

In Scotland notable stations were constructed by the North British Railway in Edinburgh in 1846, and by their rivals, the Caledonian, in Glasgow in 1848. In 1865 the Highland Railway was formed by the amalgamation of four smaller lines, and it has a collection of beautifully neat stations between Stanley Junction and Inverness. Each is worth a visit to see the trim stone buildings, latticework passenger bridges and carefully tended shrubberies and flower-beds. The economic difficulties of recent years have led to the disappearance of two fine stations — Glasgow (St Enoch) of the Glasgow & South Western, and Edinburgh (Princes Street) of the Caledonian.

Important provincial stations had their hotels, a fine example in the Jacobean style being found at Stoke on Trent (North Staffordshire Railway). The station hotel at York is a fitting partner for the famous curved trainshed, and there are fine buildings at Hull, Manchester (Central), Birmingham (GWR) and Sheffield (Midland). The hotel at Gleneagles on the former Caledonian line is justly famous.

Bristol Temple Meads. Brunel's terminus lost its importance after the Great Western and Bristol & Exeter Railways amalgamated in 1876. A new site to the south of the old station was developed and now is one of the finest in Britain. The building has an imposing tower topped by pinnacles. The three windows with mullions and transoms add to the effect.

Appleby (West) has a three-gabled building on the down platform and a waiting room on the up. Note the attractive bargeboards. The Midland had enough money to spare for wayside stations despite the expense of building their Carlisle line in 1876. The train is the up Thames-Clyde Express.

Darlington station by W. Bell (1887) has tracks for through trains on the outside, those for stopping trains being in the middle. The admirable functional plainness is relieved by Italianate buttresses.

The North Eastern Railway made certain their York station should be a worthy one. T. Prosser built it on a curve in 1877 to replace the old one within the city wall, dating from 1840 and used by the York & North Midland. There are three crescent shaped areas of glazing in the gable-end screens

ABOVE: *Audley End. Francis Thompson designed the station for the Eastern Counties Railway in 1844. There is a hipped roof and round-topped windows. The canopy is lead-covered. The porte cochere has excellent rustication. This pleasing design was for the benefit of Lords Howard de Walden and Braybroke.*

BELOW: *Battle. William Tress was a pupil of Sir William Tite and he was commissioned by the South Eastern Railway to design various stations for their line from Tunbridge Wells to Hastings. In 1852 he chose Victorian Gothic at Battle to blend with the architecture of the nearby abbey. The windows are in Decorated style with leaded lights. The roof has crenellated ridge tiles.*

13

ABOVE: *Kew Gardens buffet. Built for the London & South Western Railway in 1869 by Sir William Tite, the chief features are round-headed revealed windows and doors, a hipped roof and eaves resting on corbels.*

BELOW: *Thurso is Britain's most northerly station. The simple overall canopy dates from 1874.*

Lidlington. When the Bedford Railway was constructed in 1846, the principal landowner, the Duke of Bedford, stipulated that the stations should be ornate. Although this view was taken in 1890 the building has scarcely altered. Note the patterned brickwork and tiles hung in fishtail fashion.

SUBURBAN AND COUNTRY STATIONS

After the railway companies had built grand stations at the ends of their lines they came down to earth rather suddenly and found that there was little money left for intermediate stations. Near London, the South Eastern and the London Chatham & Dover railways were content with wooden platforms and station buildings, whereas the London Brighton & South Coast erected some good brick-built stations. The Eastern Counties Railway, never wealthy, managed to have a fine Italianate terminus at North Woolwich in 1847, and the North London, starting on a modest scale, indulged in a grand rebuilding scheme in 1873 with a whole series of excellent stations at Canonbury,

Highbury, Caledonian Road and Dalston. It is strange that the wealthy companies, like the London & North Western and the Midland, saved money by constructing very low platforms making entering or alighting from a carriage difficult for the aged or infirm. In contrast, the struggling Great Eastern, after 1862, built excellent brick stations, and in later years, such as at Hainault and Fairlop or between Edmonton and Cheshunt, supplied the public with needlessly expensive stations, although this was to their credit.

In the early days the London & Birmingham placed wretched wooden shelters for waiting passengers at their country stations, such as at Leighton

Buzzard and Wolverton. There were no facilities for comfort and even tickets were often bought elsewhere, following the stage-coach tradition. The L & BR timetables had a footnote for Wolverton passengers advising them to purchase their tickets at the Swan Hotel, Newport Pagnell, four miles away. Tickets were written by hand until Thomas Edmondson invented his ticket-printing machine in 1839, after which the idea of printing was slowly adopted by the companies. Another small concern to have artistic stations was the North Staffordshire, even at small wayside stations, whereas the mighty North Eastern often used timber.

The *porte cochere,* which is an archway at the entrance of a station to protect travellers from the weather, was adopted by many railways, as for example at Audley End, Eastern Region.

Some country buildings were above average such as Oxford (GWR), Semley (L & SWR), Aylesbury (Metropolitan) and Horley (LB & SCR). The Manchester Sheffield & Lincolnshire opened several branches in Lincolnshire in 1849 and provided notable stations at Brigg and Gainsborough, the latter being an attractive Italianate design. In the case of the Northampton & Peterborough Railway, opened in 1845, there was the advantage of having material ready to hand as almost the whole line lies in the limestone belt. J. W. Livock took advantage of this and designed some very pretty stations. Although the number of railway stations in Britain has diminished from 9,000 in 1914 to 2,500 today, there is still a vast field awaiting inspection by the enthusiast.

Buckingham (1850), with Doric columns, cornice and pediment. This was one of the stations on the Buckinghamshire Railway designed by J. W. Livock for Sir Harry Verney and the Marquis of Chandos. It was closed in 1967.

ABOVE: *Stamford. Sancton Wood was the architect for the Syston & Peterborough Railway and he produced this excellent station in 1848 in local stone. The weathervane shows the letters S & PR.*

BELOW: *Wansford on the Northampton & Peterborough Railway, perfect Jacobean by J. W. Livock, 1845. Closed by BR in 1957, the station has been reopened by the Peterborough Railway Society and the Nene Valley Railway.*

ABOVE: *Buxton, where twin stations were opened in 1863. The L&NWR came from Stockport and the Midland, seen here in 1963 four years before closure, from Millers Dale. Both were in Romanesque style with great fan windows. The Duke of Devonshire made certain stipulations and Sir Joseph Paxton's influence can be detected.*

LEFT: *Hertford East. The simple station provided by the Northern & Eastern Railway in 1843 was completely rebuilt by the Great Eastern in 1888. Note the pretty Dutch gable and windows with mullions and transoms. There are ventilators in place of the usual dormer windows.*

ABOVE: *Althorne, Great Eastern style of 1889, has tiles hung on the gables in fishtail pattern and Tudor-type chimneys. The valances are typical GER.*

BELOW: *Sandy is an example of the GNR standard country station. It is built of local gault bricks and has a stone stringcourse and round-topped windows (date 1850).*

TOP: *Alford Town, closed in 1970. The East Lincolnshire Railway preceded the GNR by opening in 1848, although the larger company worked the trains. Alford Town has this attractive arcade with Doric columns and a cornice of mutule blocks supporting a parapet with handsome finials.*

CENTRE: *Roydon. The Northern & Eastern Railway started from Stratford and reached Roydon in 1840 and Bishops Stortford in 1841. Roydon is a little gem built of timber with bow-fronted verandah and coupled columns. The rounded doorheads and the decorative valancing complete the picture and make it easy to understand why the station is listed for preservation.*

BOTTOM: *Bourne, closed in 1959. When the GNR reached here in 1860 from Essendine they purchased The Red House, a splendid Tudor residence that had belonged formerly to Sir Everard Digby, of Gunpowder Plot fame. Note the beginning of the Renaissance style in the entrance archway and the chimneys. The building was used as stationmaster's house and booking office. The Spalding & Bourne Railway came in 1866 (later the M&GNJR) to share The Red House.*

ABOVE: *Wadhurst. In 1851 the South Eastern Railway commissioned William Tress to design stations on their Tunbridge Wells to Hastings line. Wadhurst is in Italianate style with an attractive hipped roof. The brickwork is relieved by quoins and a stringcourse and the eaves are supported by mutule blocks.*

BELOW: *Dulverton, opened in 1873 on the broad-gauge Devon & Somerset Railway, which was taken over in 1901 by the GWR who had worked it since 1876, and closed in 1966. The fretted valances are worthy of high praise.*

ABOVE: *Greenwich. The original London & Greenwich Railway station of 1836 was completely rebuilt by G. Smith in 1878. He designed elegant windows with hoods resting on corbels. The appearance is enriched by the stringcourse and stone quoins. The architect chose this Palladian style to match the Queen's House nearby.*

BELOW: *Haven Street was opened on 20th December 1875 by the Ryde & Newport Railway, which became part of the Isle of Wight Central Railway in 1887. The Southern Railway took over the line in 1923 and rebuilt this station in 1926, taking care to preserve the Victorian atmosphere. Closed by British Rail in 1966, the station was reopened by the Isle of Wight Locomotive Society with 2 miles of track in 1976. This is a beautifully maintained station and the IOWLS gained the premier award in the Best Restored Station Competition held by the Association of Railway Preservation Societies in 1986.*

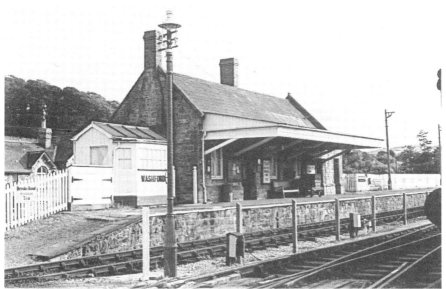

ABOVE: *Washford dates from 1874 when it was opened by the Minehead Railway. The Great Western Railway absorbed the line in 1876 and converted the track from broad to standard gauge in 1882. This is an attractive stone building with the typical GWR awning and valance. British Rail closed the line in 1971 and the West Somerset Railway reopened it in 1976.*

BELOW: *Cheddleton. The Churnet Valley Railway amalgamated with two others to form the North Staffordshire Railway in 1847 and Cheddleton station was opened on 13th July 1849. The NSR was famous for its fine station architecture and Cheddleton is no exception with walls of the local reddish stone and Jacobean-style chimneys. Although the station closed in 1965 it soon became a subject for preservation and by 1978 the North Staffordshire Railway (1978) Limited had acquired locomotives, coaching stock and a length of track. There is also an interesting NSR museum.*

ABOVE: *Loughton is a very good example of modern concrete construction. This photograph shows the double-cantilever fan-shaped concrete awning with glass bricks to improve lighting. The Eastern Counties opened their branch in 1856; steam operation was ended by the LPTB in 1948.*

CONCRETE BUILDINGS

The use of concrete on a large scale may be said to have started in 1916 when the Midland & Great Northern Joint Railway, at their Melton Constable works, prefabricated railings, slabs, steps and lengthmen's huts in that material. Shortly after, the Great Northern adopted concrete for signal posts to replace the life-expired timber ones. Railway companies were gradually converted and rapid strides were made in the 1939 war. Lack of money prevents British Rail from indulging in a wholesale rebuilding of stations, but notable examples in concrete are Twickenham, Ashford (Kent), Diss, Harlow Town and Oxford. Luton was completed by the LM & SR just as war broke out in 1939. Sometimes, as a measure of economy, a station is given a 'face-lift' as at Trowbridge.

When the London Passenger Transport Board took over London's Underground in 1933 great strides were made in rebuilding stations and opening new lines. The London Transport Board, which succeeded the LPTB in 1948, has continued the work notably where the tube lines run on the surface in the outer suburbs. A good example is Hatton Cross, and at Heathrow the modern station is being further developed by London Regional Transport (Underground).

Digswell viaduct, Welwyn. The Great Northern Railway employed William Cubitt as civil engineer, and he had this imposing structure ready for the opening of the line on 7th August 1850. This was in spite of the severity of the winter of 1849/50 when frost held up construction for several weeks. The viaduct is 1560 feet in length and 90 feet in height. The line was electrified by overhead catenary in 1976 and an electric multiple unit train is seen crossing.

BRIDGES, VIADUCTS AND TUNNELS

Part of our great legacy from the Victorian engineers lies in the major achievements in crossing rivers and boring through mountains. There are hundreds of bridges carrying loads far greater than those envisaged by the designer, giving proof of their worth a century after their construction. Mention must be made of Robert Stephenson's Conway and Menai Straits tubular bridges (1850), and Brunel's flat arch at Maidenhead (1839), Chepstow (1852) and Saltash (1859). Stephenson's square-section tubular Menai bridge lasted until 1970 when the spans were damaged by fire and replaced. Brunel's were a combination of arch and suspension and gave wonderful service; Chepstow was replaced in 1962 and Saltash has been strengthened.

For sheer size, one must turn to Scotland. The firths of Tay and Forth presented formidable obstacles to the North British Railway, and at first passengers had to embark on ferry boats to cross the waters which were far from smooth in winter. In 1878 the Firth of Tay was crossed by a bridge built to the designs of Thomas Bouch. Unfortunately a terrible gale on 28th December 1879 brought down part of the bridge with a train on it and 73 passengers perished. There were many reasons for the failure, but poor Bouch, as engineer, had to carry the responsibility. A new bridge was commenced in 1882 and that is the one we now use when going to Dundee. Over the Forth an amazing cantilever bridge was built to the plans of Sir John Fowler and

Robert Stephenson had to carry the London & Birmingham line over the river Great Ouse near Wolverton in 1838. The lovely six-arch viaduct has three small arches at the approaches each end. Stephenson found time to attach columns to his buttresses and give them decorative capitals. The viaduct was widened from two to four tracks in 1881.

Benjamin Baker and opened in 1890.

There is a great range of stone or brick-built viaducts anywhere between Inverness and Brighton. The mountains and valleys of Scotland presented a challenge which was accepted with alacrity. On the West Highland Railway Charles Forman's great viaducts near Tyndrum should be seen and, paradoxically, the motorist has a better view than the passenger in the train. Robert Stephenson's genius is shown at the Royal Border Bridge, Berwick, and at the Newcastle High Level bridge, both ready in 1850. Brunel completed the Wharncliffe viaduct near Hanwell in 1837, and this is as strong today as when built. In the far west his viaducts have disappeared because the superstructure was of timber. On the journey to Brighton, just before Haywards Heath, the train crosses Rastrick's fine Ouse viaduct (1841); it has been embellished by Mocatta with four pavilions at each end.

Whereas bridges were admired, tunnels were often deplored and had to be disguised to please neighbouring landowners. Mocatta added castellated turrets to Clayton tunnel on the London & Brighton, and Brunel decorated Twerton tunnel, between Bath and Bristol, in the same manner. At Audley End the Eastern Counties Railway was compelled by Lord Braybrooke to adorn the tunnel porticoes with expensive elaborations.

Barmouth viaduct is 800 yards long. It had been proposed by the Aberystwyth & Welsh Coast Railway in 1861 but was not opened until 3rd June 1887. This was by the Cambrian Railways Company which had absorbed the A & WCR. The viaduct contained a good deal of timber in its construction and this was mostly replaced by steel in 1899. In the 1980s the remaining timber had to be renewed owing to damage by the parasite Teredo navalis. There is a pedestrian footway on the east side.

RIGHT: *Brunel saw to it that his viaduct near Bath blended with the surroundings. It is built with medieval-style battlements, church-type buttresses and arches. The GWR was opened throughout in 1841.*

St Pancras water tower. This is an excellent design with seven stone and brick linked arches forming a blind arcade. The base is a stepped plinth. William Barlow, who built the St Pancras train shed in 1868, was responsible for this water tower, showing that a civil engineer can also be an able architect.

RIGHT: *Brunel's masterpiece is the Saltash (Royal Albert) bridge over the river Tamar. Erected in 1859 it carried the 'Castle' class easily, but the heavier diesel engines necessitated some strengthening in 1968.*

ABOVE: *The Forth Bridge, 1890, the well-known triumph of Sir John Fowler and Benjamin Baker.*

RIGHT: *The first bridge over the Tay was built in 1878 and was seriously damaged during a gale on 28th December 1879. The replacement bridge was opened in 1887, and this view of it also shows the foundations of the first bridge.*

BELOW: *At Carmarthen the GWR bridged the river Towy with a structure of plate girders, when renewing the 1852 work. Also shown is a typical GWR signal gantry.*

Porthmadog. The Festiniog Railway opened in 1836 for slate traffic but not until 1865 for passengers. The station therefore dates from that time. Unfortunately passenger traffic ceased in 1939 and freight in 1946. The Festiniog Railway Society reopened for passenger trains in 1955 and reached Blaenau Ffestiniog in 1982. The station buildings have been considerably extended since 1955 to include offices, booking hall, shop, refreshment rooms and a museum.

RAILWAY MISCELLANY

When the Railways Act (1921) was drafted there were still 123 separate companies in England, Wales and Scotland. It can therefore be understood what a diversity of design there would be with regard to goods warehouses, engine-sheds, signal-boxes and signals, mileposts and gradient posts. Goods warehouses were usually of brick or stone, depending on locality, with large doors at each end with a single track running through to serve a platform. Frequently there was a manually operated crane. Engine-sheds were purely functional but might have patterns in the brickwork to relieve the uniformity of long side walls. The ends were normally open, cold in winter, and floors were of concrete with inspection pits. The smoke and steam escaped from louvres in the roof, the design of which would vary from railway to railway.

There was such a great variety of signal-boxes and signals that an adequate description would fill a book. The usual construction for a signal-box was brick or stone for the ground floor, which contained the rods and interlocking apparatus, and timber and glass above, to provide the best view for the signalman. At night there was only one small lamp to illuminate the train register. Until 1923, with the exception of experiments at Victoria and Paddington, all semaphores moved in the lower quadrant. The horizontal position required the driver to stop, and he could proceed if the arm was lowered through about 45 degrees. The stop signals were painted red with a white band on the side facing the trains, and white with a black band on the reverse side. The Midland chose to have a white spot for many years, but came into line about 1910. The Great Northern, Taff Vale and others used the 'somersault' signal which moved away from the post to show line clear. After the Grouping on 1st January 1923 all the companies except the Great Western adopted upper quadrant signals, but colour-light signals are now bringing uniformity to the whole system.

Even mileposts varied considerably, and an experienced traveller would know at a glance, if on the East Coast route, just when he had left the Great Northern metals for the North Eastern. With regard to fencing, there was no mistaking the Midland's sloping palings or the Great Western's strands of wire supported by Brunel's bridge rail cut down to form posts.

This is a brief summary of a fascinating subject and it is intended that the gaps which are evident in the text shall, in some measure, be filled by the photographs. The important thing is that the reader shall be so stimulated as to wish to go and see for himself.

BELOW LEFT: *North Eastern signal-box, Shildon, on the day of the great steam locomotive parade, 31st August 1975.* BELOW RIGHT: *L&NWR signal-box, Market Harborough.* BOTTOM: *Great Northern signal-box. Great Western engine. No. 7029 'Clun Castle' at Everton in 1967 brings back memories of 1925.*

PROMINENT VICTORIAN ARCHITECTS
AND THEIR WORK

Andrews, G. T.: York station 1840; York & North Midland, York & Scarborough.
Ashbee, W.: Norwich Thorpe.
Baker, William: Broad Street, NLR 1865.
Barlow, William: St Pancras train shed and water tower 1868.
Barnes, F.: Ipswich & Bury Railway 1846.
Barry, C. E.: Great Eastern Railway Hotel, Liverpool Street.
Barry, E. M.: Charing Cross and Cannon Street hotels 1864 etc.
Bell, W.: Darlington, Hull (Paragon) 1887 etc.
Beasley, S.: Gravesend Central 1849.
Berkeley, G.: Fenchurch Street 1854.
Bidder, G. Parker: North Staffordshire Railway 1849.
Biddle, Charles: Midland Railway 1868.
Breakspear, W. H.: London & Croydon Railway 1836.
Brunel, I. K.: Great Western, Bristol & Exeter, South Devon, Cornwall, West
    Cornwall, South Wales etc, 1835 onwards.
Cooper, E. A.: Birmingham New Street.
Cubitt, Lewis: King's Cross station and hotel 1850 onwards.
Cunningham, J.: Liverpool Lime Street 1871.
Dobson, J.: Newcastle Central 1850.
Dockray, R.: Kenilworth and Leamington 1844.
Driver, C. H.: Midland Railway 1857 onwards.
Edis, Colonel R. W.: Great Central Railway, Marylebone Hotel 1900.
Fowler, John: Metropolitan Railway 1863.
Fox, C. and J.: Great Central Railway 1895 onwards.
Green, Benjamin: Newcastle & Carlisle, Newcastle & Berwick, Great North of
    England Railways, 1839 onwards.
Hardwick, Philip: Euston station and Doric propylaeum, Birmingham Curzon Street,
    Euston hotel 1835 onwards.
Hardwick, P. C.: Paddington Hotel 1854; Euston Great Hall.
Hawkshaw, Sir John: Charing Cross and Cannon Street stations, London; Liverpool
    Tithebarn Street; 1864 onwards.
Horne, E. H.: rebuilding of North London Railway stations 1873.
Hunt, H. A.: Stoke-on-Trent station, North Staffordshire Railway and others, from
    1850.
Hurst, W.: Stamford East (Marquess of Exeter's Railway) 1856.
Isaacs, L. H.: Holborn Viaduct station, London Chatham & Dover Railway 1877.
Livock, J. W.: Trent Valley Railway 1847; Buckinghamshire Railway 1850; North-
    ampton & Peterborough Railway 1845.
Mocatta, David (pupil of Sir John Soane): London & Brighton Railway 1841.
Paxton, Sir Joseph: Midland Railway, Buxton station 1863.
Penson, T. K.: Shrewsbury 1849.
Pritchett, J. P.: Huddersfield 1847.
Prosser, T.: Leeds (North Eastern Railway) 1869; York 1877.
Pugin, A. W. N.: North Staffordshire Railway 1849.
Rastrick, J. U.: London & Brighton Railway 1841.
Roberts, H.: London Bridge (South Eastern Railway) 1844.
Sanders, J. H.: Bath Green Park, Somerset & Dorset Joint Railway 1870.
Scott, Gilbert: St Pancras hotel 1873.
Shelmadine, Henry: Liverpool Exchange 1886.
Smith, G.: Greenwich, South Eastern Railway 1878.
Stephenson, Robert: Chester station, Conway, Menai Straits, Newcastle and Royal
    Border bridges, from 1835 to 1850.

Thompson, Francis: Audley End and Cambridge, Eastern Counties Railway; North Midland Railway 1840; Chester & Holyhead Railway 1849.
Tite, Sir William: London & Blackwall Railway 1840; and for the London & South Western Railway, Nine Elms 1838, Kew Gardens and Southampton 1840, Hampton Court, Windsor and Weybridge 1849; also Lancaster & Carlisle Railway.
Tress, William: stations on the South Eastern Railway, e.g. Wadhurst, Robertsbridge and Battle, 1851 onwards.
Trubshaw, Charles: Midland Railway, Manchester Central, Leicester 1892.
Wilson, E. D.: Great Eastern Railway, Liverpool Street 1874.
Wood, Sancton: Eastern Counties Railway, also Syston & Peterborough Railway 1848.
Wyatt, Sir Matthew Digby: Great Western Railway, Paddington 1854.

FURTHER READING

Allen, C. J. *Great Eastern Railway*. Ian Allan, 1956.
Allen, C. J. *North Eastern Railway*. Ian Allan, 1974.
Anderson, R., and Fox, G. *Pictorial Record of London Midland and Scottish Railway Architecture*. Oxford Publishing Company, 1985.
Anderson, R., and Fox, G. *Stations and Structures of the Settle and Carlisle Railway*. Oxford Publishing Company, 1985.
Beckett, D. *Stephenson's Britain*. David and Charles, 1985.
Betjeman, Sir John. *London's Historic Railway Stations*. John Murray, 1972.
Biddle, G. *Great Railway Stations of Britain*. David and Charles, 1986.
Biddle, G. *Victorian Stations*. David and Charles, 1973.
Biddle, G., and Nock, O. S. *The Railway Heritage of Britain*. Michael Joseph, 1984.
Clarke, L., and others. *Aspects of Railway Architecture*. Brunel Engineering Centre Trust, 1985.
Conder, F. R. *The Men Who Built the Railways*. T. Telford, 1984.
Ellis, C. Hamilton. *British Railway History*. George Allen and Unwin, 1956.
Ellis, C. Hamilton. *London Brighton and South Coast Railway*. Ian Allan, 1971.
Ellis, C. Hamilton. *Midland Railway*. Ian Allan, 1974.
Gladwin, T. W.; Neville, P. W.; and White, D. E. *Welwyn's Railways*. Castlemead Publications, 1985.
Hoole, K. *North Eastern Branch Termini*. Oxford Publishing Company, 1985.
Hoole, K. *Railway Stations of the North East*. David and Charles, 1985.
Jackson, A. A. *London Termini*. David and Charles, 1985.
Karan, P. *Great Western Branch Line Termini*. Oxford Publishing Company, 1985.
Lambert, A. J. *Nineteenth Century Railway History through the Illustrated London News*. David and Charles, 1984.
Potts, C. R. *Great Western Stations*. Oxford Publishing Company, 1984.
Signalling Study Group. *The Signal Box*. Oxford Publishing Company, 1986.
Simmons, J. *St Pancras Station*. George Allen and Unwin, 1968.
Vaughan, A. *Pictorial Record of Great Western Railway Architecture*. Oxford Publishing Company, 1984.
Wrottesley, A. J. *Midland and Great Northern Joint Railway*. David and Charles, 1970.